Assignments 2

PPY PRESS - LONDON

Published by the PPY PRESS
Press Photographers Year Ltd.
52-58 Shorts Gardens
London WC2H 9AN
call us: +44(0)20 7870 1255
email us: info@theppy.com
visit us: www.theppy.com

Produced by Tim Bishop and Dillon Bryden
Design: SMITH. Lesley Gilmour
www.smith-design.com

Origination: Euro Digital, Passau, Germany
Printing: Passavia, Passau, Germany
Binding: Conzella, Pfarrkirchen
Printed in Germany on 170 gsm BVS matte
and 300gsm Invercote G acid-free papers.

-

ISBN 978-0-9556019-0-3

Assignments 2

hajj mina stampede, hamas win majority, mozart 250th, turin olympics, leyte mudslide, al askari bombing, itunes 1 billionth song, melbourne games, smoking ban, avian flu, brunel 200th, java earthquake, montenegro, operation summer rains, kuwaiti women vote, italy win world cup, mumbai bomb attacks, google buys youtube, vista, scream recovered, polonium-210, schumi retires ,thai coup d'état, saddam executed, wii, hamster crashes rocket car, baiji extinct.

The Press Photographer's Year

Walt Disney cut the ribbon at the opening of Disneyland with the haunting concern: "What if nobody comes?" We worried at the launch last year of the inaugural Press Photographer's Year, that there would be no pictures, no entrants, and no book. But now at the end of it's second year, this is a competition that has gone in eighteen months from a photographers' talk around a café table on London's South Bank, to the largest national press photography competition in Europe. It's not been easy. It's often long, hard labour – and largely volunteer labour, at that. So why do we do it?

It's because, at last, there's a real appetite for a genuine, honest showcase for the finest press photography in Britain.

Press photography, strangely, doesn't get a good press, by and large. So much of it doesn't even make the paper. It may be a technical problem - pictures arriving too late for edition. It may that a news story loses prominence, and drops down page, or even off the page. It may be an editorial decision that the pictures are just too strong. It doesn't matter how long those pictures took to get, how far the photographer traveled, how long was the wait, how dangerous the job.

The truth is that while some assignments bring pictures that splash across the front pages, others produce well-observed, but gentle images from unpromising subjects that lift dull inside pages. Some bring a very real personal danger, and many can be sheer tedium. It is a struggle to make something new, different, eye-catching, from a routine assignment, shot so many times before. Then there are long hours of waiting around when nothing happens, to be ready for the split-second when it does. Above all this stands the hardest taskmaster, The Newspaper, offering the photographers increasing uncertainty of employment. Even staffers are concerned about how long they will remain employed, and freelancers unsure of their next shift.

It was against this background that some members of the British Press Photographers' Association (BPPA) began to dream of developing a competition. There would be a named jury to view all the entries. They would judge from hard copy prints, not a log on to some web gallery. The emphasis would not be on winning prizes, but on producing an outstanding record of the year, through the eyes of the some of the most brilliant press photographers in the world. The very best images would go on exhibition at the Royal National Theatre. There would be a book. It meant finding a sponsor with vision, who could grasp exactly what it was we were trying to achieve: a lasting showcase for our newspapers' often most poorly recognised contributors, with photography itself at the very core.

Actually none of this formed a very promising start. No budget, expensive ideas, and organisers, enthusiastic, but with no actual experience of running a competition, let alone designing one from scratch. The deadlines were mad, the long hours scary, the calling-in of favours sometimes pushing a little hard. It was a process of persuading busy people with little time, to give some of that time to you, for free, in return for being part of something new. A change.

There are low points. Some shocks came in the chase for funding. There were promises that brought nothing. Smiles while people in the photography industry explain this 'not quite right for them'. There was some resistance to the words 'press photographer'. Advice was that we needed to be a little more creative, to come up with something that sounded less like 'person on TV chasing celebrities' and more 'creating with light'. Perhaps instead of the Press Photographers' Year, it could be 'Visual Journalism Year'. Then there are those who came brandishing a shopping where it seemed that an invitation only 'knees-up' was rather higher up the agenda than a celebration of the photography .

We were fortunate to find sponsors who share the PPY's vision of photography. For the second year running Canon UK provides the PPY with core funding. They have proved much more than our key sponsors. Cari Bibb and Graham Smith have helped us with ideas, suggestions, and often bringing their enthusiasm, encouragement and expertise when it was most needed.

Having built the first website that photographers could upload, and edit their entries on line, Tom Scott and James Crossett of Talking Pixels have worked long and hard to redesign and reinvigorate the PPY website for 2007. Loxley's Chris Kay handled our print orders in impossible deadlines, both for the judging and the exhibition. Our designer Stu Smith, assisted by Lesley Gilmour, has again brought his own unique stamp to the whole project in the book and exhibition design. The Royal National Theatre's John Langley has been a vital and most forgiving supporter to our project, allowing us to use the facilities for our jury to deliberate over the entries, and then later in the year hosting our Expo Day and exhibition. We also owe very special thanks to Alastair Mackeown and Brian Murphy for their support at a critical time.

Our jurors, led by twice World Press Photo chair Roger Hutchings, gave their time freely to the hardest of edits. Composed of top photographers in their own right, Double Pulitzer prize winner Horst Faas, BPPA founder John Downing, BPPA Chairman Jeff Moore, Geraint Lewis, Nobby Clark, and David Caukin, the jury examined every single one of the six thousand images, over two days of thought-provoking debate about what makes a press image classic or hackneyed, and what lifts one shot into the realms of significance.

But behind it all is Dillon Bryden, who never seems to tire. He thrives on tracking and solving the many crises as they arise. It is his dogged determination, his creativity, which has brought the photography competition for photographers by photographers to life for another year.

So what exactly do I do? I have the irritating role of whispering, sometimes shouting in Dillon's ear: Stop spending money. We just can't do that. How much will this cost? We need to do this by when? Are you mad? Are we mad? We hope you will agree, it has been well worth the struggle.

tim bishop
co-founder of the press photographer's year

contents

sean smith THE GUARDIAN
Ali Sha'ita, 12, tries to comfort his mother. Their
extended family was wounded when the three vans
in which they were travelling were hit by an Israeli
missile in Tyre, Lebanon. They were evacuating from
the village of Et Tiri, on the road from Tebnine.
23rd July 2006.

observations on press photography: the message, and the role of the photographer as a messenger

roger hutchings
chairman of the 2007 jury

As you turn the pages of this second book of the Press Photographer's Year it is obvious that, as a group of pictures, they amount to a dossier of evidence about events, political issues, meetings, celebrities, relationships, appearances, and landscapes - each with its own implications. Some are of international significance, such as those covering the invasion of Lebanon, others touch moments of daily life, which, should we reflect, may lead us to think, there but for the grace of God go I. Christian Sinibaldi's picture of a migrant in Calabria, on page 70, is a fine example. There are pictures that reveal bare facts and emotions, and pictures that insinuate a more complex situation, as in the curious image on page 73, by Peter Nicholls of Jack Straw timidly guiding Condoleeza Rice towards the cameras. Some pose the question why or ask how dare they. Others condemn our behaviour, warn us for the future, ask us to respond before it is to late: Clare Kendal's picture of dumped skidoos on page 40. The critical evidence is gathered, then presented to an audience where it becomes a transaction between the witness and the viewer. The photographer proclaims, 'Look at this - what do you think'; the viewer is asked to trust the picture. Of course! Pictures never lie! We know that to be a fallacy but in general we do not scrutinize pictures in a newspaper or magazine with any degree of scepticism. We take it for granted that what the picture says or shows is accurate or true, more so if the image appears in a venerated publication. But is it actually the picture we trust, or its respectable context? I would suggest, for instance, that we would be more believing of a picture in the Manchester Guardian or the New York Times than of one in the Zimbabwe Herald or the former state monopolized newspaper Pravda. We tend to have more faith in an image that is brought into the public domain via an infrastructure that we consider trustworthy. Journalism at its best is an honourable practice; at its worst it is a scurrilous activity, or propaganda. As far as photography is concerned much depends on the principles and scruples of the originator of the photograph.

*

To trust the photograph we must trust the photographer, or rely on the editors who are presenting the image to us to have confidence in its provenance. A photograph can, very simply, be made to mislead. The famous black and white photograph of Ku Klux Klan members by W. Eugene Smith, who is often regarded as the photojournalists' role model, is printed in such a way that the white participants appeared to have black faces, and although the intention to ridicule the Klan was obvious, the picture is not factual.

In our digital age it has never been easier to amend, enhance, add or remove the content of an image: a practice common and accepted in fine art photography but a cardinal sin in journalism. The potency of reportage, documentary or photojournalistic photography depends above all on its authenticity, and that in turn depends on the integrity of the photographer and the creed that he or she adheres to. The publication relies on the honesty of the photographer, as do we the audience being informed.

So vital is the relationship of trust between a news organization and its consumers that Reuters dismissed a photo-editor who was found to have passed a manipulated picture of the recent war in South Lebanon for distribution. It goes without saying that the freelance photographer concerned was also struck off their books. Similarly in 2003 a Los Angeles Times staff photographer was fired after it was discovered that he had combined two images into one picture from the war in Iraq. The Times went to great lengths to explain to readers how it happened and what their ethical policies are regarding the alteration of photographs. It is unsurprising that editors tend to trust photographers who have a track record and whose work has been endorsed by time. There are different sides to any story but a photographer's obligation is to challenge himself about the meaning of what he is looking at or the issues he is exploring, so as to be able to say when he presents the work that, having assessed the facts, the way I am telling the story, what I am leading you to believe, is the way that I saw it. Rigorous enquiry is a prime duty of the news photographer and sensible photographers frequently question themselves over the ethics and accuracy of how they are documenting a story.

*

There have been many widely seen 'set-up' pictures, directed by the photographer, but presented as reportage. One noted photographer once said to me, 'Show me an award winning picture and I'll show you a set-up.' It was said in jest but has a shred of truth to it. A set-up, while fabricated, is often used as a metaphor to tell a real story for which an illustration is desperately needed, or to satisfy the pre-conceived notions of a picture editor. It provides an efficient way of getting ideas across, but is not truth and the audience should be told so that it can be seen for what it is.

With this burden of integrity in mind, the recent wave of citizen journalism and the deluge of amateur digital images which daily assail news organizations have become an issue of some concern, since the origins and facts will constantly need to be verified as unimpeachable. It seems likely that there will be more cases like the faked pictures alleging abuse of Iraqi prisoners by British soldiers.

The designation photojournalist carries with it an implication of probity.

The responsibility is squarely on the photographers' shoulders; there are no short cuts when it comes to telling the truth and being true to oneself. It's part of the contract we sign with ourselves when we elect to pursue our profession. There is no better philosophy than to adopt the motto: 'Truth needs no ally'. If the photographer has a duty to his audience he similarly has one to his subjects. When I was a novice photographer, it was instilled in me that we were all ambassadors for one another and that my behaviour should make it easy for the next photographer to come along and be welcomed. There should be confidence but never a sense of self-importance. I think we always need to tread gently. Never trample people, nor forget the extreme generosity of strangers to us news gatherers as we intrude into their lives, often in circumstances of loss or despair.

*

As you journey through these pages of arresting pictures think a little about the men and women who created them. They required courage, ingenuity, tenacity, and belief in their medium. There is a general perception that the photographer leads a life of glamour and financial gain. It is certainly not the case with photojournalism. The men and women who have produced the work you are looking at often live a testing existence of physical danger and financial hardship to record what will become the history of our times. What challenges did Sean Smith have to overcome to capture the picture of a bloodied family in South Lebanon? Would you even know how to get into southern Lebanon with the airport bombed, the borders closed, the Israeli navy patrolling the coast? And would you brave the journey to Tyre with the prospect of a few thousand tons of state-of-the-art incoming explosive devices landing on or near you?

This important image of the tragedy unleashed upon innocent civilians because of the misguided Israeli invasion leaves the viewer gasping with despair at the horror of war and the ongoing futility of the Middle East conflict. Reflecting upon an image of such carnage, and seeing the expression of the wounded boy leaves one with the grim realization that, as acts of violence beget retaliation, this is all going to happen again.

*

Leaving aside the darker aspects of our vocation, I wonder whether sports photographers are challenged by the same self-imposed obligations. I think not, though I believe that like all photographers they are searching for the essential truth of the spectacle before them. By and large, there is no obvious political element to their work, yet there is no doubt that the electric mood captured in Tom Jenkins' photograph of Wayne Rooney's red card moment, on page 115, accurately reflects feelings about England's performance in the recent World Cup, and therefore represents the lost hopes and frustration of a whole nation of football fans - and that may well have socio-political ramifications.

Sports photographers need to be masters of technique. Having been sent once by the *Observer* to cover a First Division football match I quickly found out how incompetent I was in comparison with the sports specialists with their lightning reflexes. The following Sunday, I saw that Chris Smith of the *Sunday Times* had taken the most stunning picture, and for the life of me I couldn't believe that I had been at the same event. There are many examples of excellent sports photography here: for instance, Alex Livsey on page 116, has captured Ronaldo's character laid bare, oblivious to everything around him, lost in self-revelation, with his team mates as his triumphal lieutenants. Michael Steele's aerial view of a pole-vaulter, on page 105, reminds us of that a thoughtful, meticulously planned approach is vital to the sports photographer's art, while on the final spread, Dan Towers dramatic picture of a lone yacht in the hands of the elements makes one shudder. It is awesomely beautiful, full of the menace of the cruel sea, and confirms the notion that long-distance ocean yacht racers must be amongst the bravest, toughest people. Yet also ask what lay behind the image. How did the photographer get the picture? Where was he - on a similar boat? In a helicopter?

The sports picture is not necessarily about peak-of-the-moment action. Scott Barbour's black and white panorama of snow polo in Switzerland on page 116 shows how elegantly a landscape rendition can capture the essence of a sporting event. Whereas one might expect the photographer to shoot tighter, looking for drama, the delicate, painterly picture of small figures on horseback performing their ritual battle beneath the wintry slopes of the Alps suggests that sometimes it's good to stand back and take in the scene.

*

Putting aside thoughts about this particular collection of pictures, it is worth speculating about the future of press photography. The press photographer is a messenger despatched to gather information to enlighten, inform, correct and admonish. The resulting pictures can be sophisticated and complex visual essays or striking single images crafted from the photographer's relentless pursuit of a story, coupled to rigorous attempts to make the pictures as good as possible.

Press photography in Britain has an important cultural role that is not sufficiently acknowledged by society in general, or the arts community in particular, especially when compared to the status it has in other countries like France or America. It is surely easier to practice as a contemporary art photographer with only oneself to answer to, than to serve the deadline-focused editors of a mainstream publication or photo agency, while at the same time nourishing and placating one's own creative hunger.

It looks as though the press photographer is morphing into a multi-media practitioner producing video, sound and stills from one camera. That is simply evolution and adjusting to market conditions. If anything, we should be glad of the opportunity to use different media that offer the choice of the best way to tell a particular story. The next generation of photographers may look back and think it rather curious that there was a time when people *only* took pictures - and possibly think how limiting it was. On the other hand, there is no escaping the compelling, lingering nature of the still image. Once seen, it may never go away. I think that Peter Nichols' photograph, on page 15 of a child whose face has been lacerated by shrapnel after an Israeli bombing raid in South Lebanon will always be lodged in my memory. It is intimate, and as a viewer I have become implicated in her tragedy and wonder about her future. If I had seen the girl's plight reported in video news footage, I doubt I would remember so acutely.

first prize: photo essay

peter nicholls THE TIMES
As the ceasefire commenced, one of the first families to walk through the rubble of the southern suburbs of Beirut, in the area of the last devastating bombing raid, was Samira Haydova with one of her young daughters, while recovery and rescue attempts continued at the site. 14th August 2006.

peter nicholls THE TIMES
A woman and injured child sit in front of destroyed
buildings and vehicles in the southern suburbs
of Beirut, as people return to collect belongings
following the ceasefire between Israel and
Hezbollah, and a heavy bombing campaign
on the area by Israel. 15th August 2006.

peter nicholls THE TIMES
Ghadir Shaito, 15, recovers in a Beirut hospital after
being seriously injured in Israeli air raids on her
village in southern Lebanon. 27th July 2006.

A young man grieves over the dead of the recent bomb attack on an apartment block in the southern Shiyah district. Fifty six people died and were late buried in a mass grave. 9th August 2006.

Lebanese protestors attack the UN Economic Commission for Western Asia headquarters in downtown Beirut, after the killing of civilians in Qana by the Israelis. 30th July 2006.

As the ceasefire commenced, one of the first families to walk through the rubble of the southern suburbs of Beirut, in the area of the last devastating bombing raid, was Samira Haydova with one of her young daughters, while recovery and rescue attempts continued at the site. 14th August 2006.

yonathan weitzman REUTERS
Israeli settlers clash with Israeli security forces
in the evacuation of the West Bank settlement of
Amona. More than 200 policemen and settlers
were injured in the clashes. 2nd January 2006.

yonathan weitzman REUTERS
An Israeli soldier rests on ammunition boxes while an Army 155 mm mobile artillery fires into southern Lebanon from a position on the frontier in Zaura. 15th July 2006.

yonathan weitzman REUTERS
An Israeli soldier rests before going into south Lebanon. 10th August 2006.

sean smith THE GUARDIAN
Scared children flee Aitaroun village, south Lebanon, in a car after being caught up in hostilities between Israel and Hezbollah. 1st August 2006.

adrian fisk
Seven bombs ripped through the first class carriages of the mainline railway to Bombay, injuring 700 and killing 200. Kashmiri separatist groups were blamed for the attacks. A blood-stained trolley lies outside the morgue at the Sion hospital where the victims of the bombings were taken. 11th July 2006.

peter nicholls THE TIMES
The Palestinian Prime Minister Ismail Haniyeh, surrounded by heightened security, attending the 19th anniversary rally of HAMAS in Gaza city. This was his first appearance in public since returning from his Middle East fund-raising trip. 15th December 2006.

matt dunham AP
Women attempt to salvage possessions from the remains of a building in the southern suburbs of Beirut, which was destroyed by an attack from Israeli forces during the 34-day Israeli-Hezbollah conflict. The densely populated residential area was bombed repeatedly by Israeli forces during the conflict. 27th August 2006.

youv galai
Company Commander Roy Nahari, right, talks to seriously wounded medic Tom Shechter, injured in a friendly fire incident in the village of Ainata, on the outskirts of the southern Lebanon town of Bint Jbail. 12th August 2006.

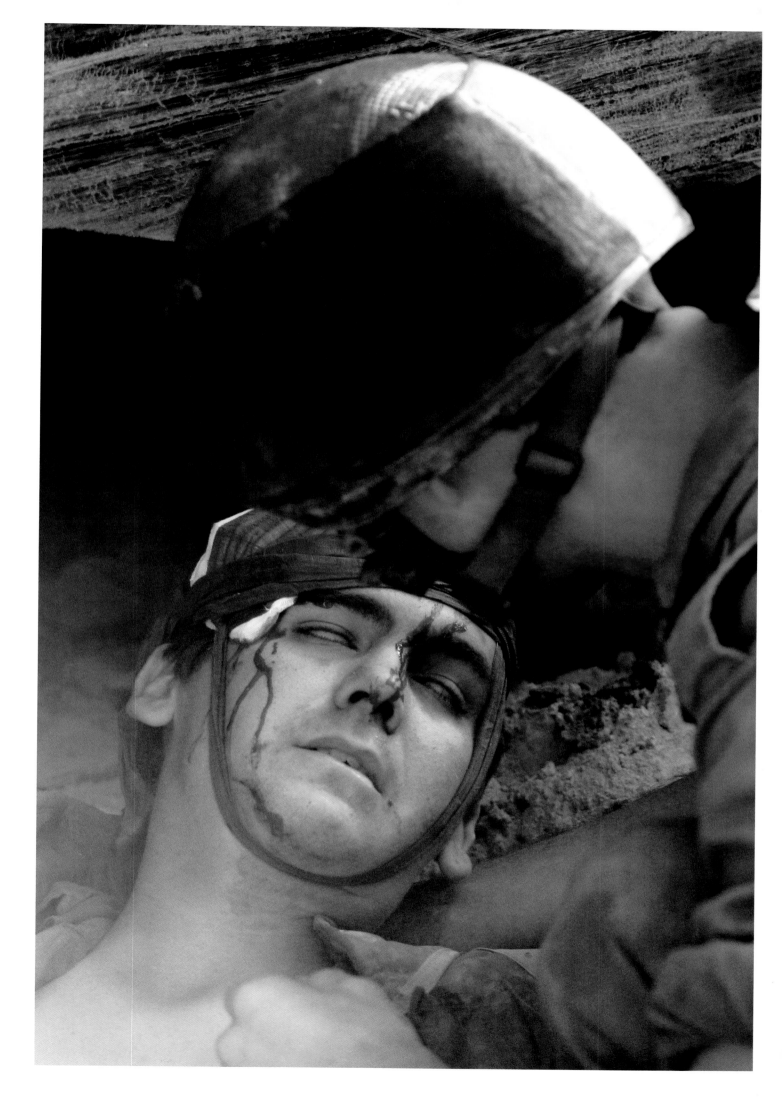

richard wainwright CAFOD

The town of Mongbwalu in the Democratic Republic of the Congo (DRC) is home to one of the world's richest gold fields but the people remain trapped by a cycle of violence and poverty. This area has been plagued by conflict for decades as different armed groups struggle to win command of the gold. 14th January 2006.

daniel berehulak GETTY IMAGES
Young Iraqi boys play soccer amongst protective
blast walls in Baghdad, Iraq. It was here on 14th
October, 2005 that two suicide bombers drove their
vehicles, within a minute of each other, into the
perimeter of the Al Hamra hotel compound,
attempting to breach the walls. The explosions
destroyed a nearby apartment block, killing at least
eight Iraqi civilians, including two children. A recent
report released on September 1 from the Pentagon
stated the number of deaths in Iraq has increased by
1,000 people a month over the previous quarter, to
more than 3,000 violent deaths each month. 2nd
September 2006.

first prize: news

sean smith THE GUARDIAN
Soldiers from 2nd platoon Delta Company, 327
Infantry Regiment, 101st Airborne squad, and the
Iraqi army out on an early morning air assault
to arrest four wanted men - three were caught.
The captured men are blindfolded or hooded and
wear plastic handcuffs. Forward Operating Base
McHenry. Hawijah, Iraq. 21st June 2006.

paula bronstein GETTY IMAGES
An elderly protester is taken off the street by riot
police as she tries to convince them to let her
stay during a demonstration. Nepal's opposition
groups are calling for a restoration of democracy
from King Gyanedra's royalist regime and vow to
continue their protests until he steps down. Violent
clashes became a regular occurrence between
pro-democracy groups and the government's forces.
King Gyanedra's royalist government ordered
a curfew, cutting phone lines and internet access
and arresting anti-government activists while a ban
on protests continues to anger Human Rights
organizations. Nepali men chant as water cannons
are shot at them during a demonstration protesting
against the rule of King Gyanedra in Kathmandu.
24th January 2006.

paula bronstein GETTY IMAGES
Injured demonstrators huddle together after tens of
thousands of Nepalese protesters are beaten back
by armed police as they tried to march on the streets.
24th January 2006.

justin sutcliffe
Slobodan Milosevic's body travels to the funeral site
in his former home town of Pozarevac. A mourner
rolls up a poster of Milosevic as the crowds start to
disperse following the passage of the cortege.
18th March 2006.

casper dalhoff

E-Huset is a nursing home for socially unadapted alcoholics in Copenhagen, Denmark and funded by the local government.

39 people over the age of 45 live in E-Huset in 'De Gamles By' (the City of the Old). Everyone is highly addicted to alcohol and has given up the fight of getting out of the addiction. All walks of life are represented in E-Huset, and every person has his or her own story about what it feels like to let someone down or to be let down yourself. There is a Christmas party in the common room and before long, as the band begins to play the old classics from the 'good old' pub days, the dance floor gets busy. 14th December 2006.

simon dack BRIGHTON ARGUS

Audrey Peat (left) from Brighton who was
threatened with arrest for non-payment of her
local Council Tax, with her sister Violet Chamberlain
who requires around-the-clock care. Audrey's
husband Leslie was earlier arrested and is awaiting
a court appearance. 6th July 2006.

richard mills THE TIMES

British National Party Chairman Nick Griffin and his minders goad anti-fascist supporters from a window at Leeds Crown Court at the start of his trial. He had been charged on several counts of inciting racial hatred, but was later acquitted. 16th January 2006.

peter muhly AFP

Security officials remove a handgun from the grip of former Protestant paramilitant Michael Stone (centre) at Stormont Parliament buildings in Belfast, as he tries to disrupt the first session to discuss power-sharing plans for Northern Ireland. 24th November 2006.

john giles PA

WPC Teresa Milburn (centre) who was shot and wounded when her partner WPC Sharon Beshenivsky was murdered during a robbery in Bradford is comforted by Colleagues at a Memorial Service in Bradford. 18th November 2006.

sang tan
Culled chickens and eggs being removed for incineration from the Norwich Road poultry farm at North Tuddenham in Norfolk. 7,500 chickens were culled after the H7N3 strain of bird flu virus was detected in the farm, near to Whitford Lodge poultry farm where 35,000 chickens were culled earlier after a similar outbreak of the virus. 30th April 2006.

angela catlin
Cite Soleil in Haiti is one of the world's most notorious slums and has a population of over 400,000 people. The area is controlled by several gang leaders and is in effect a war zone. The extreme violence has turned it into a no-go area for security forces or police. A young boy walks by a river of raw sewage and rubbish: a playground of filth. 28th November 2006.

timothy allen AXIOM
A judge examines the entrants in the British Homing World 'Show of the Year' at the Blackpool Winter Gardens. It is considered the Crufts of the racing pigeon world. 20th January 2006.

tony bartholomew
The silhouette of Peter van Vliet, who uses biodynamic techniques to produce organic vegetables and herbs at the 650 acre Botton Village on the North Yorkshire Moors where he is a farm manager for the project, run by the Camphill Village Trust. 18th December 2006.

daniel berehulak GETTY IMAGES
Highly radiated vehicles used to dump concrete and water during the 1986 catastrophe lay in a field near the village of Rosoha in Chernobyl, Ukraine. More than 30 military helicopters flew over the burning reactor. They failed to put out the fire with 2400 tonnes of lead and 1800 tonnes of sand. Tanks, helicopters, and all terrain vehicles from the Soviet Union's Red Army were left in this dump due to their high levels of radiation. 31st January 2006.

daniel berehulak GETTY IMAGES
A podium lies in the middle of an abandoned school gymnasium in the city of Pripyat near Chernobyl, Ukraine. Prypyat and the surrounding area will not be safe for human habitation for several centuries. Scientists estimate that the most dangerous radioactive elements will take up to 900 years to decay sufficiently to render the area safe. 25th January 2006.

clare kendall
A skidoo graveyard on the outskirts of Ivujivik in the Canadian province of Nunavik. The Inuits have largely abandoned dog sleds as their main form of transport in favour of snowmobiles, which are not recyclable, and contribute to global warming. As the sea ice thins, accidents are becoming commonplace, as unlike dog teams, skidoos have no innate ability to know if the ice is safe to cross. 12th April 2006.

timothy allen AXIOM
From a series on 'A Monk's Life' in the remote
Himalayan Kingdom of Bhutan. 30th September
2006.

christopher furlong GETTY IMAGES
An Israeli 155mm artillery gun fires as part of the barrage against Hezbollah targets in South Lebanon continues. 20th July 2006.

simon roberts
Largely ignored by the international community, the war in Chechnya is now Europe's longest-running and bloodiest conflict. No one knows exactly how many civilians have died since 1994 but the number runs into the tens of thousands. The city of Grozny, the republic's only urban and professional centre, still lies in ruins more than a decade after the fighting started. Here Grozny inhabitants shop in one of the central markets amongst the ruins of apartment blocks. Grozny, Chechnya. 15th March 2006.

christopher furlong GETTY IMAGES
A lone Israeli woman carries on with life and
sunbathes on a deserted beach in the northern
Israeli town of Nahariya during a lull from the
onslaught of Hezbollah rockets. 21st July 2006.

angela catlin
A grandmother and her granddaughter, along with her children, wait to be re-housed as her home in the Govan area of Glasgow is to be demolished. 23rd August 2006.

len copland WESTERN GAZETTE
School girls arrive for the highlight of their school year: the summer prom. On exiting their chauffeur driven Hummer limousine the girls used the reflection in the side of the car to check their hair and makeup. 7th July 2006.

nils jorgensen REX FEATURES
Every day, about 30 million journeys are taken in Greater London, of which 6.3 million are by bus, 3 million by Tube, 1.4 million by rail, and 7 million on foot. Having recently stopped using his car, due to London's recent Congestion Charging scheme, the photographer found that it has provided a great opportunity for photography. 21st July 2006.

nir elias REUTERS
A North Korean soldier stands guard at an army installation on the bank of the Yalu River, 37 miles north of the North Korean town of Sinuiju, opposite the Chinese border town of Hekou. 20th October 2006

peter nicholls THE TIMES
A Brazilian soldier, part of the UN force present in Haiti, patrols in the Cite Militaire area of the capital, Port-au-Prince. 2nd February 2006.

daniel berehulak GETTY IMAGES
Endurance swimmer Lewis Gordon Pugh swims in
the Thames River past the Houses of Parliament
on his way to become the first person to swim and
complete the entire length of the River Thames.
4th August 2006.

following spread

cathal mcnaughton PA
An Eastern White pelican eats a pigeon in
St.James's Park, London. 24th October 2006.

kirsty wigglesworth AP
One of thousands of dead flamingoes on the dry
lake bed in Lake Nakuru National Park, Kenya.
The number of flamingoes living on the lake has
declined dramatically; a number of factors has
been blamed including the receding waters of the
lake, and pollution. 9th November 2006.

lenny warren EVENING TIMES
A thrush tends to her chicks at a nest built on
traffic lights on Eglinton Street in Glasgow, Scotland.
11th May 2006.

jeff j mitchell GETTY IMAGES
Head stalker Peter Fraser and his hunt party stop
to look for stags in Glen Callater on the Invercauld
Estate near Braemar, Scotland. 29th September
2006.

jeff j mitchell GETTY IMAGES
Head stalker drags a stag at Milstone Cairn in Glen
Callater on the Invercauld Estate near Braemar,
Scotland. 29th September 2006.

jeff j mitchell GETTY IMAGES
The shot stag being towed back to the Invercauld
Estate near Braemar, Scotland. 29th September
2006.

jeff j mitchell GETTY IMAGES
A pony man takes a shot stag out from Milstone
Cairn in Glen Callater on the Invercauld Estate near
near Braemar, Scotland. 29th September 2006.

jeff j mitchell GETTY IMAGES
A man skins a stag's head at Auchallater farm on the
Invercauld Estate near Braemar, Scotland. 29th
September 2006.

andrew parsons PA
Edward Timewell, a member of the Atlantic Whale
Foundation, splashes water onto a Northern Bottle-
Nosed whale as it swims in the River Thames in
London. It is the first sighting of the species on the
river since records began. 20th January 2006.

clare kendall
Sea ice in the Hudson Bay off the Canadian province
of Nunavik, breaking up prematurely due to the
effects of global warming. 4th April 2006.

dan charity
A spectator at Royal Ascot struggles to cope with the wind. 21st June 2006

scott barbour GETTY IMAGES
Racegoers make their way home after the final day of Royal Ascot at the Ascot Racecourse in Berkshire, England. The event has been one of the highlights of the racing and social calendar since 1711, and the royal patronage continues today with a Royal Procession taking place in front of the grandstands daily. 24th June 2006.

richard pohle THE TIMES
Lance Corporal Lewis Montague of the Black Watch regiment walks through the shadows of the Thiepval memorial on the 90th anniversary of the start of the Battle of the Somme as he attempts to find the name of his great-uncle. There are 70,000 names inscribed on its walls as a memorial to those soldiers whose bodies were lost and never recovered in the Somme area during the First World War. 1st July 2006

timothy allen AXIOM
The Layap Tribe live in a remote part of north west Bhutan in the Himalayas on the China Tibet Border - their village is 5 days' walk from the nearest town and their culture remains untouched by the outside world. 28th September 2006.

phil wilkinson TSPL
A young girl waits her turn for an eye test at the Bo government hospital in Sierra Leone where Sightsavers International run the clinic. 29th September 2006.

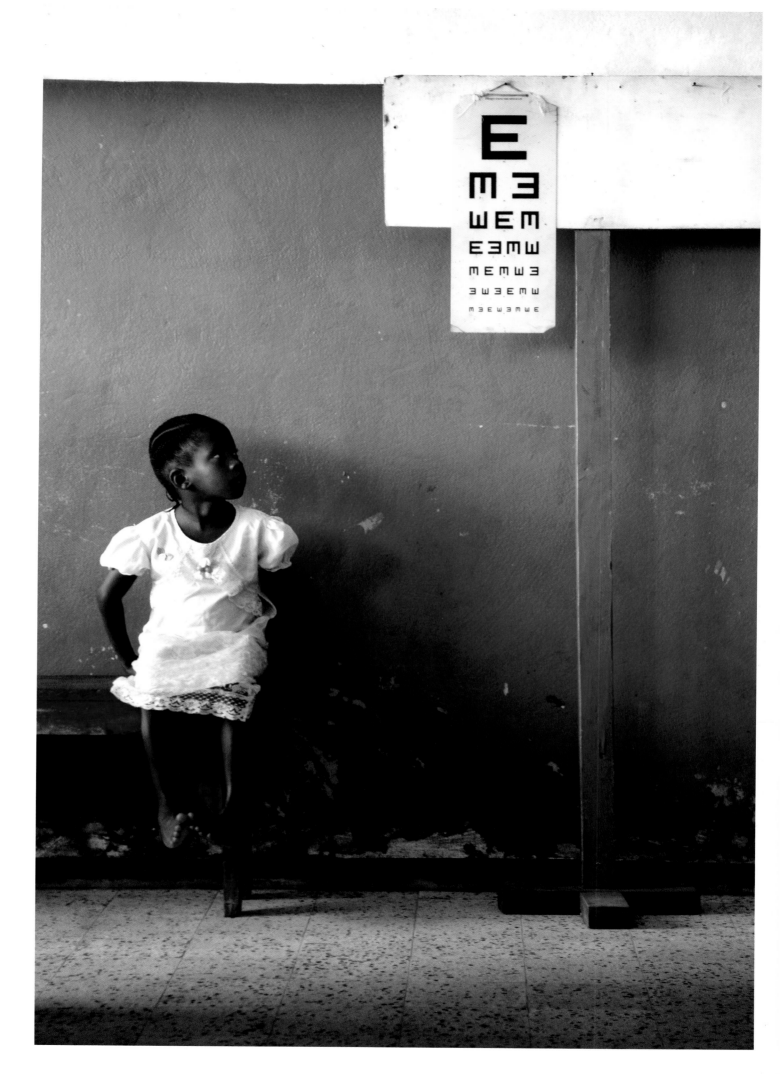

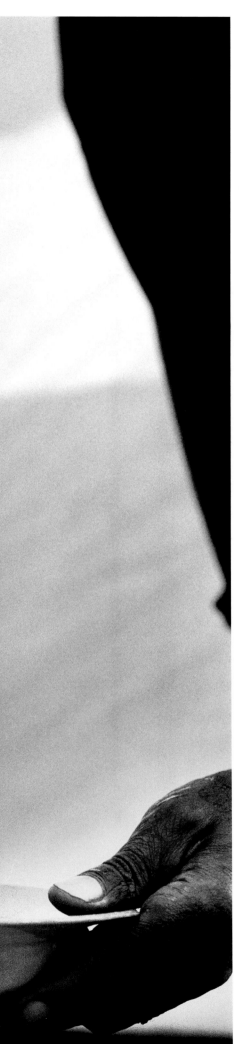

bruno stevens COSMOS

Francisca, a patient at the Cazenga MSF operated cholera field clinic in Luanda, Angola. Between February and June 2006, more than 30,000 people were infected with cholera in Angola's worse outbreak ever. More than 1300 died. 21st May 2006.

ahikam seri PANOS PICTURES

Ayalah Tadesah, a homeless man also known as Yonathan, photographed in his current refuge, an abandoned house in central Jerusalem, where he has been living for the last four years. Poverty rates in Israel are on the rise during the last few years, as the state moves fast from its socialist past into a capitalist future. 20th February 2006.

peter sandground

Gordon Brown, who is strongly tipped to be the next Prime Minister, on a visit to businesses in his home constituency of Fife in Scotland. 16th June 2006.

shaun curry

Then British Foreign Secretary, Jack Straw about to give an emergency statement in the Foreign Office in London to comment on the explosions that occurred at al-Askari Mosque in Samarra, Iraq earlier that morning, effectively destroying its golden dome and severely damaging one of Shi'ite Islam's holiest sites. 22nd February 2006.

kirsty wigglesworth PA

Britain's Deputy Prime Minister John Prescott sits on the stage at the Labour Party conference during the opening session in Manchester, England. 24th September 2006.

ben gurr THE TIMES
Michael Howard, the former leader of the
Conservative Party, is reflected in the stopper
of a water carafe whilst being interviewed about
the forthcoming party conference in his office at
Portcullis House, Westminster. 28th September
2006.

adrian dennis AFP
Britain's Prime Minister Tony Blair glances upwards
as he leaves Downing Street in London. Blair
was to vow to resign in a year's time to prevent
an increasingly damaging crisis from engulfing
his government, a spokesman said, but calls for
him to go sooner remain. The embattled leader has
repeatedly refused to discuss his departure plans.
7th September 2006

graeme robertson
The British Prime Minister's wife Cherie Blair in 10
Downing Street. 27th February 2006.

graeme robertson
The controversial British R&B vocalist Mark Morrison photographed in Barbados. 30th January 2006.

following spread

andre camara
This young man in Johannesburg is the happiest employee of this English company's subsidiary there. Saved from the streets, this is his first job. He washes the other employees' cars and helps with other duties. Now he can help his family with the regular pay the job provides every month. 6th April 2006.

felix clay
Mrs Boyd and a friend Mr J.D Kirkwood enjoy a very mild October afternoon with the washing out at Greeves Park Lodge, Lancaster. 18th October 2006.

richard wainwright CAFOD
A young artisan gold miner carries raw quartz rock to the town of Mongbwalu in Ituri district, Eastern Congo. Despite working in one of the richest gold fields in the world the population have been plagued by conflict and poverty for decades. Many children cannot afford to go to school so mine from a very young age to help their family survive. 12th January 2006.

paul haigh
Freshly slaughtered pigs on their way to the morning markets in Hoam Kiem, Hanoi, Vietnam. 28th September 2006.

christian sinibaldi

Many of the migrants who have come to Calabria in southern Italy live in conditions that would not even meet the UN's basic minimum standards for refugees in camps in war zones. About 80 migrants are squatting in a derelict factory on the edge of Rosarno. Samia, from Ghana, is one of them. He cannot work at the moment because he is still suffering from a car accident in Naples a few months ago. 3rd December 2006.

john angerson
Former Ulster Unionist Party leader David Trimble at his home in Lisburn, Northern Ireland. 15th May 2006.

peter nicholls THE TIMES
Jack Straw guides US Secretary of State Condoleezza Rice from her car to the entrance of the BAe systems factory at Blackburn, Lancashire: the first in many of their stops of her tour of the north-west of England. 31st March 2006.

phil wilkinson TSPL
The photographer Albert Watson, photographed
during a break in a photoshoot of the Scottish Opera
production of Der Rosenkavalier. 31st July 2006.

max mumby
A tearful Duchess of Cornwall leaving the Holy Trinity Church at Stourpaine in Dorset after the funeral of her father, Major Bruce Shand. 16th June 2006.

bruno vincent GETTY IMAGES
Marina Litvinenko, the wife of poisoned former Russian KGB spy Alexander Litvinenko, walks through Highgate Cemetery after his funeral. Litvinenko's death on 23rd November has been linked to the radioactive element Polonium 210. Scotland Yard are treating the case as murder whilst detectives continue their inquiries in Moscow. 7th December 2006.

**first prize: the arts
cathal mcnaughton** PA.
Sarah Rew (centre) as Alice joins Mrs Tiggywinkle (left) and Peter Rabbit (right) on a roof garden overlooking St Paul's Cathedral in Dowgate Hill, London. The children's storybook characters were helping the English domestic tourism industry launch its latest campaign to inspire families to discover the real locations that appear in their favourite books. 4th September 2006

sam furlong
Members of animal charity PETA stage a naked protest in the middle of Bristol city centre to highlight the plight of fish caught in nets. 5th October 2006

graeme robertson
A retrospective exhibition of the American minimalist artist Dan Flavin held at the Hayward gallery in London. 18th January 2006.

cate gillon THE HERALD
A scene from *Inferno*, an adaptation from translations of Dante's Inferno which is written and directed by Andy Arnold, performed at The Arches in Glasgow. 13th March 2006.

max mumby
A tearful Duchess of Cornwall leaving the Holy Trinity Church at Stourpaine in Dorset after the funeral of her father, Major Bruce Shand. 16th June 2006.

bruno vincent GETTY IMAGES
Marina Litvinenko, the wife of poisoned former Russian KGB spy Alexander Litvinenko, walks through Highgate Cemetery after his funeral. Litvinenko's death on 23rd November has been linked to the radioactive element Polonium 210. Scotland Yard are treating the case as murder whilst detectives continue their inquiries in Moscow. 7th December 2006.

**first prize: the arts
cathal mcnaughton** PA.
Sarah Rew (centre) as Alice joins Mrs Tiggywinkle (left) and Peter Rabbit (right) on a roof garden overlooking St Paul's Cathedral in Dowgate Hill, London. The children's storybook characters were helping the English domestic tourism industry launch its latest campaign to inspire families to discover the real locations that appear in their favourite books. 4th September 2006

sam furlong
Members of animal charity PETA stage a naked protest in the middle of Bristol city centre to highlight the plight of fish caught in nets. 5th October 2006

cate gillon THE HERALD
A scene from *Inferno*, an adaptation from translations of Dante's Inferno which is written and directed by Andy Arnold, performed at The Arches in Glasgow. 13th March 2006.

mimi mollica CORBIS
The view from the Italian Customs Police helicopter
'Volpe 219' of a small boat full of illegal immigrants
spotted few miles east of Lampedusa Island, off the
coast of Sicily. Every year thousands depart from the
Mediterranean coasts of Africa, trying to reach
Europe through Sicily. The Italian authorities are
struggling to keep the situation under control and
are constantly patrolling the area, and end up
rescuing many of the immigrants. Overcrowded, and
ill prepared boats make fatalities inevitable, and
many bodies are found washed up on the shore.
This boat was carrying thirty five immigrants from
North Africa and Eritrea, who were later picked up.
25th June 2006.

graeme robertson
The Ocean Spray cranberry harvest in Boston, USA.
14th October 2006.

roger bamber
Artist Chris Drury mows his 'Finger Maze', a 38m by
30m impression of his own fingerprint, in the grass
of Stanmer Park, Falmer, Sussex. The work was
commissioned by the Brighton & Hove Arts 'Making
a Difference' initiative to bring art outside for more
people to enjoy. 22nd June 2006.

wattie cheung
Justin Hawkins of rock group, The Darkness, playing
live at the SECC in Glasgow, Scotland.
12th February 2006.

abbie trayler-smith
A businessman arrives for work in the financial
district of Beijing, China. 13th May 2006.

graeme robertson
Sculptor Ron Mueck with his latest work; 'A Girl'
as it is taken out of its mould in his studio in North
London. 11th July 2006.

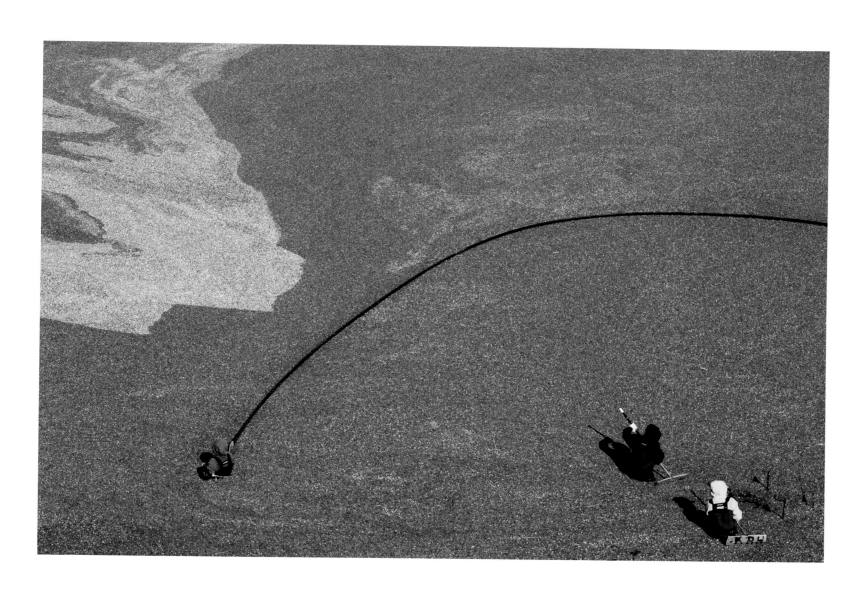

rosie hallam

The French theatre group Royal de Luxe staged the biggest piece of free theatre ever seen in the capital when they performed 'The Sultan's Elephant' over the Bank Holiday weekend in London. 5th May 2006.

casper dalhoff

On 26 April 1986 an explosion took place at the Chernobyl nuclear power plant, in the present Ukraine. Since then the region and the world have not been the same. In the days following the catastrophe, thousands of people were evacuated from the city of Pripyat, around which most of the radioactive fall-out was centred. Twenty years on, the city is deserted. 57 people died as a direct result of the accident. The UN organisations estimate that a total of 4,000 people will die from the longer-term consequences. 27th March 2006.

andrew baker
Tube trains from the Underground's Jubilee Line stored at the Burford Road Depot in Stratford, east London. 12th October 2006.

following spread

lewis whyld PA
The Queen smiles as she passes her grandson Prince William whilst inspecting the graduates at the Sandhurst Military Academy passing out parade. 15th December 2006.

mark stewart
A cavalry officer's horse showed the 80 year old Queen no respect as it butted her during a prize giving ceremony at the Royal Windsor Horse Show. The Queen showed no ill effects from the swipe, and was soon smiling again. 13th May 2006.

alan davidson
The Queen inspects The Queen's Cup at the Cartier
Queen's Cup polo day at The Guards Polo Club at
Smiths Lawn Windsor. 18th June 2006.

dave shopland
HRH The Princess Royal at Sandown Park
racecourse to present the prizes on Grand Military
Gold Cup Day. 10th March 2006.

eddie mulholland
Two of the world's biggest ballet companies went head to head in London where for the first time the Mariinsky and Bolshoi ballet companies both staged performances at the same time, Ekatarina Kondaurova from the Mariinsky and Nikolai Tsiskaridze from the Bolshoi were on hand to show Mayor of London Ken Livingstone some of their moves. 13th July 2006.

harry borden
Sir Paul McCartney the singer-songwriter, during the recording of his album 'Ecce Cor Meum' (Latin for Behold My Heart) at Abbey Road Studios, London. 17th March 2006.

alan davidson
Helen Mirren relaxes at the after-show party for 'The Queen' at the Venice Film Festival. 2nd September 2006.

dylan martinez REUTERS
American actress Sharon Stone arrives for the world premiere of 'Basic Instinct 2' at The Vue Cinema in London's Leicester Square. 15th March 2006.

john ferguson DAILY MIRROR
American rock chick Pink in the back of her limousine in Paris, on her way to the launch of her new album, 'I'm Not Dead'. 28th March 2006.

gareth cattermole GETTY IMAGES
American actress Sandra Bullock arrives at the UK Premiere of 'The Lake House' at The Vue Cinema in London's Leicester Square. 19th June 2006.

andrew milligan PA
Sigourney Weaver at the Dominion Theatre in
Edinburgh for the premiere of her film 'Snow Cake'
during the Edinburgh International Festival.
15th August 2006.

lee thompson
Bruce Forsyth at the 18th hole at the Northern Rock
Allstar golf tournament at the Celtic Manor in
Newport, Wales. 28th August 2006.

bob martin
Ski-jump practice at the Winter Olympics in Turin,
Italy. 20th February 2006.

toby melville REUTERS
Horses competing in the Cheltenham Festival are
ridden out in the morning on the course's gallops.
The annual four-day National Hunt race meeting is
one of the highlights of the global racing calendar,
with nearly 500 horses racing. It is attended by
250,000 spectators. 13th March 2006

dominic lipinski NOTTINGHAM EVENING POST
Noah Sible competes in the First Timers category
at the United Kingdom Bodybuilding Fitness
Federation Championships at the Royal Concert
Hall, Nottingham. 8th October 2006.

michael steele GETTY IMAGES
Abdulla Ghanim S.M. Saeed of Qatar competes
in the Men's Pole Vault Final during the 15th
Asian Games at the Khalifa Stadium Doha, Qatar.
10th December 2006.

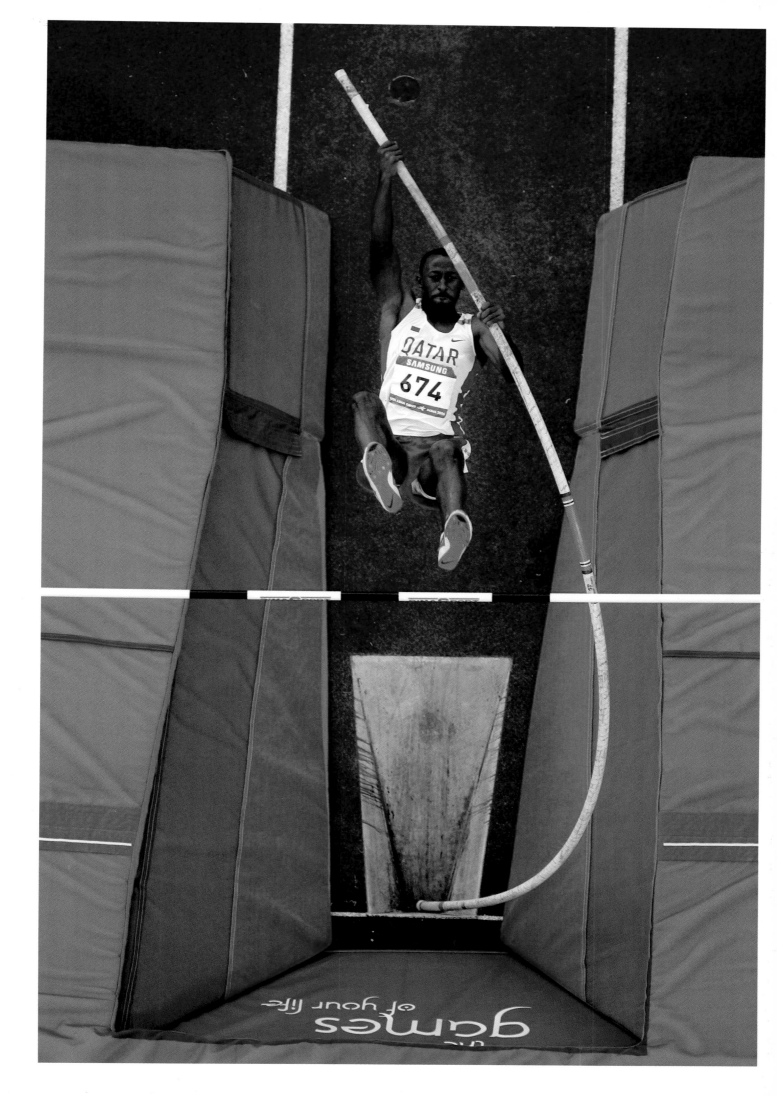

first prize: sports action

peter sandground
Dario Ojeda, a windsurfer for the Canary Islands, battles 60 to 80mph winds during the Red Bull Storm Chase at Machrihanish, on Scotland's Mull of Kintyre. Dario had travelled the length of the British Isles looking for perfect storm conditions in order to make jumps of up to 40 feet above the waves. 26th October 2006.

clive mason GETTY IMAGES
Australian Chris Atkinson, driving for the Subaru
World Rally Team, in action during the ninth stage
of the Wales Rally GB in Llandovery, Wales.
2nd December 2006.

julian finney GETTY IMAGES
A man paints his house as the peloton makes its
way through the village of Sheriffhales on the
Wolverhampton to Birmingham stage of the
Tour of Britain cycle race. 1st September 2006.

chris ison PA
Competitors in the 75th Round The Island Race
bunch up at The Needles lighthouse on the western
tip of the Isle of Wight as the winds drop. The race
is the oldest of its kind in the world with around
1,800 yachts of all sizes and abilities vying to be
the fastest to make the 50 mile clock-wise
circumnavigation of the island. 3rd June 2006.

tom jenkins THE GUARDIAN
The British Women's Bobsleigh Team round the
notorious 'Kriesel Loop' whilst competing at the
World Cup Final in Altenberg, Germany.
27th January 2006.

colin mearns THE HERALD
The French team manager Raymond Domenech on his phone in an empty stadium after his team was beaten 1-0 by Scotland in their Euro 2008 Qualifier at Hampden stadium, Glasgow. 7th October 2006.

alex livesey GETTY IMAGES
Cristiano Ronaldo of Portugal celebrates with his team mates after scoring the winning penalty in a penalty shootout at the end of the FIFA World Cup quarter-final match between England and Portugal played at the Gelsenkirchen Stadium in Germany. 1st July 2006

laurence griffiths GETTY IMAGES
Peter Crouch of Liverpool exchanges words with Noe Pamarot of Portsmouth during their Barclays Premiership match at Anfield. 29th November 2006.

scott barbour GETTY IMAGES
The 22nd Cartier Polo World Cup on Snow in St.
Moritz, Switzerland. The matches are played on the
frozen surface of Lake St. Moritz, against the
backdrop of the Swiss Alps. The lake needs to freeze
to a depth of at least 30 centimetres to support the
weight of the players and spectators safely.
29th January 2006.

rebecca naden PA

Spain's Rafael Nadal celebrates his victory during
the fourth round of The All England Lawn Tennis
Championships at Wimbledon. 3rd July 2006.

robert hallam

Swimmer Melanie Marshall during a training session
at Loughborough University. 18th December 2006.

richard heathcote GETTY IMAGES
Danilo Alipan of The Philippines (top) spikes the ball past Lee Gyu Nam of South Korea during the Sepaktaraw Men's Double Preliminary matches in the Al-Sadd Indoor Hall during the 15th Asian Games in Doha, Qatar. 11th December 2006.

laurence griffiths GETTY IMAGES
A Togo fan looks dejected after the FIFA World Cup Group G match between Togo and Switzerland at the Stadium Dortmund in Germany. 19th June 2006.

jeff j mitchell GETTY IMAGES
Callum Garret dives in the mud during the first ever UK Swamp Soccer tournament in Dunoon, Scotland. Swamp Soccer originates from Finland and is fast becoming an alternative sport with tournaments taking place all over the world. 1st July 2006.

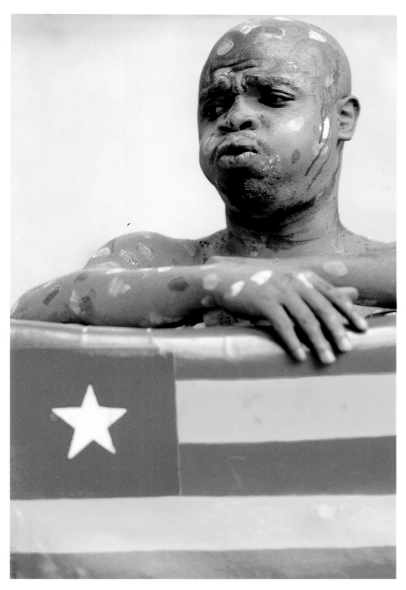

toby melville REUTERS
England and Germany soccer fans clash in Stuttgart city centre. Despite sporadic outbreaks of violence between rival supporters, the 2006 World Cup finals were hailed as a successful and mainly hooligan-free tournament. 24th June 2006.

michael regan ACTION IMAGES
France's Zinedine Zidane reflects on a missed chance during the World Cup Final in Berlin. Italy eventually beat France on penalties after Zidane was sent off. 9th July 2006.

alex livesey GETTY IMAGES
Fabio Cannavaro of Italy lifts the World Cup trophy following his team's victory in a penalty shootout at the end of the FIFA World Cup Final match between Italy and France at the Olympic Stadium in Berlin, Germany. 9th July 2006.

tom jenkins THE GUARDIAN
Wayne Rooney is shown the red card during the England's FIFA World Cup Quarter Final match with Portugal at Gelsinkirchen in Germany. 1st July 2006.

peter macdiarmid GETTY IMAGES
An English football fan is detained under a billboard near Schlossplatz in Stuttgart, Germany during the FIFA World Cup. 24th June 2006.

dan towers ON EDITION

Bernard Stamm fights for survival in hurricane force winds in the Bay of Biscay on the second day of the VELUX 5 Oceans which started in Bilbao, Spain.

The VELUX 5 Oceans is the longest and toughest event, for any individual in any sport. By the end in Fremantle, western Australia, the skippers will have sailed 30,000 miles of ocean alone, facing all the extremes that nature can throw at them. 23rd October 2006.

acknowledgements

The Press Photographer's Year would like to thank all the photographers who submitted photographs for the competition and for kindly allowing us to reproduce them in this book and at the accompanying exhibition.

The copyright for each of the photographs published in this book is held by the individual photographer with the exception of the following publications and agencies.

The Press Photographer's Year are very grateful to them for their permissions.

Action Images; 123.
Agency France Presse, 34 bottom, 64 bottom.
Associated Press, 22, 50 bottom.
Brighton Argus; 33.
Daily Mirror; 97 top.
Evening Times; 51.
Getty Images; 25, 28, 29, 38, 39, 43 top, 44, 48, 52-53 all, 57 left, 75 right, 86 top, 97 bottom, 100, 105, 108, 109, 114-117, 120, 121 both, 122 bottom, 124.
The Glasgow Herald; 77 bottom, 113.
Goff Photos; 99, 101.
The Guardian; 6, 20 top, 26, 112, 125.
Newsquest Media Group; 86 bottom.
On Edition; 126.
Press Association; 35, 50 top, 54, 63, 76 top, 90, 98, 110, 118.
Reuters; 18, 19 both, 47, 96 bottom, 103, 122 top.
Rex Features; 46 bottom.
The Scotsman; 59, 74.
The Times; 12-17 all, 21, 47 bottom, 73.
Western Gazette; 44 top.

All the copyright holders have asserted their moral rights under the UK Copyright Designs & Patents Act 1988.

The Press Photographer's Year would not have been possible without the generous support of Canon Cameras. We would like to thank Cari Bibb and Graham Smith at Canon UK for their dedication to the project.

We would also like to thank the following people for their time, their support and valuable assistance during The Press Photographer's Year.

the 2007 Jury
Roger Hutchings (Chairman)
David Caulkin
Nobby Clark
John Downing MBE
Horst Faas
Geraint Lewis
Jeff Moore

at TalkingPixels.co.uk
Tom Scott, James Crossett

at SMITH
Stuart Smith, Lesley Gilmour

at the National Theatre
Nicholas Hytner, John Langley, Laura Hough, Anna Wells, Hannah Wright, Paul Jozefowski, Paul Kenah

at Passavia & Euro Digital
Elmar Steubl, Michael Wallrapp, Sandra Kössl

at Loxley Colour
Christopher Kay, Robert Orr

a special vote of thanks must go to
Alastair Mackeown
Brian Murphy

thanks also to
Julien Allen, Simon Bainbridge, Colin Breame, Hugo Burge, Carole Butcher, Melissa DeWitt, Graeme Dimmock, Victoria Forrest, Adam Gahlin, Colin Hayward, Tony McGrath, Stuart Morcom, Donal Ogilvie, Victoria Routledge, Paul Sanders, Sabine Schmidt, Katie Scott, Diane Smyth, Tom Stoddart, Rob Taggart

The accompanying exhibition was held at the National Theatre's Lyttelton Foyer between 16th June and 28th July 2007 and was printed by Loxley Colour, Glasgow

The inaugural PPY Expo Day took place in the Lyttelton Theatre on 22nd June 2007.

entrants for 2007

Bruce Adams
Jason Alden
Timothy Allen
Roger Allen
Odd Andersen
Brian Anderson
Kirsty Anderson
Julian Andrews
John Angerson
Helen Atkinson
Richard Austin
Bob Aylott
Andrew Baker
Roger Bamber
Fraser Band
Scott Barbour
Anna Barclay
Jane Barlow
Tony Bartholomew
David Bebber
Julien Behal
Natalie Behring
Sean Bell
Daniel Berehulak
Andy Blackmore
James Boardman
Jon Bond
Harry Borden
Mauro Bottaro
Shaun Botterill
Anna Branthwaite
James Breeden
Paula Bronstein
Sarah Lucy Brown
Philip Brown
Kelvin Bruce
Terence Bunch
Jason Bye
Andre Camara
Richard Cannon
Matt Cardy
Angela Catlin
Gareth Cattermole
Paul Chappells
Dan Charity
Grenville Charles
Dave Charnley
Wattie Cheung
Daniel Chung
James Clarke
CJ Clarke
Felix Clay
Philip Coburn
Phil Cole
Ian Cooper
Len Copland
Glenn Copus
Vicki Couchman
Jez Coulson
Steve Cox
Michael Crabtree
Shaun Curry
Simon Dack
Casper Dalhoff
Jules Dann
Brian David Stevens
Alan Davidson
Jason Dawson
Simon Dawson
Carl de Souza
Simon de Trey-White
Peter Dench
Adrian Dennis
Anthony Devlin
Matthew Dickens
Nigel Dickinson
Kieran Dodds
Kieran Doherty
Matt Dunham

Nic Dunlop
Hazel Dunlop
Andrew Dunsmore
Nir Elias
Paul Ellis
Stuart Emmerson
James Emmett
Jonathan Evans
Matt Faber
John Ferguson
Julian Finney
Adrian Fisk
Andrew Fox
Sam Frost
Chris Furlong
Sam Furlong
Yoav Galai
Andy Garbutt
John Giles
Cate Gillon
Martin Godwin
Anna Gordon
Charlie Gray
Claire Greenway
Spencer Griffiths
Laurence Griffiths
Ben Gurr
Paul Haigh
Andy Hall
Rosie Hallam
Robert Hallam
Paul Harding
Rebecca Harley
Richard Harris
Graham Harrison
Mark Harrison
David Hartley
Richard Heathcote
Sean Hernon
Andrew Higgins
Jack Hill
Stephen Hird
David Hoffman
David Hogan
Zann Huizhen Huang
Richard Humphries
Christopher Ison
Christopher Jackson
John James
James O Jenkins
Tom Jenkins
Baz Jennings
Bob Johns
Ian Jones
Nils Jorgensen
Terry Kane
Anna Kari
Clare Kendall
Eddie Keogh
Ady Kerry
Ross Kinnaird
Dan Kitwood
Simon Kreitem
Amit Lennon
David Levene
Karoki Lewis
Dominic Lipinski
Alex Livesey
Michael Lusmore
Peter Macdiarmid
Alex Macnaughton
Toby Madden
Thomas Main
Mike Marsland
Robert Martin
Dylan Martinez
Clive Mason
James McCauley
Andrew McConnell

John D McHugh
David McHugh
Cathal McNaughton
Colin McPherson
Colin Mearns
Toby Melville
Andrew Milligan
Richard Mills
Jane Mingay
Philip Mingo
Jeff J Mitchell
Clara Molden
Mimi Mollica
Mike Moore
Brendan Moran
Peter Muhly
Eddie Mulholland
Max Mumby
Simon Murphy
Rebecca Naden
Max Nash
Leon Neal
Jeremy Nicholl
Peter Nicholls
Ian Nicholson
Phil Noble
Russ Nolan
David Parry
Andrew Parsons
Richard Pelham
Dan Phillips
Ryan Pierse
Tom Pietrasik
Tom Pilston
Mark Pinder
Lefteris Pitarakis
Christopher Pledger
Suzanne Plunkett
Richard Pohle
Jonathan Pow
Lucy Ray
Michael Regan
Kiran Ridley
Simon Roberts
Graeme Robertson
Tim Rooke
Clive Rose
Stefan Rousseau
Peter Sandground
David Sandison
Tom Saunderson
Oli Scarff
Jamie Scott-Long
Jeremy Selwyn
Dwayne Senior
Ahikam Seri
Martin Shields
Dave Shopland
John Sibley
David Silverman
Julian Simmonds
Mike Simmonds
Jamie Simpson
Derek Simpson
Christian Sinibaldi
Guy Smallman
Sean Smith
Tim Smith
Matt Sprake
Michael Steele
Bruno Stevens
Mark Stewart
Bettina Strenske
Akira Suemori
Justin Sutcliffe
Sang Tan
Peter Tarry
Edmond Terakopian
Andrew Testa

Andy Thomas
Lee Thompson
Layton Thompson
Allan Titmuss
Chris Tofalos
Dan Towers
Abbie Trayler-Smith
Graham Trott
Neil Turner
Dominick Tyler
Toby Vandevelde
Eva Vermandel
James Veysey
Bruno Vincent
Richard Wainwright
James Wakefield
Michael Walter
Lenny Warren
Zak Waters
Geoff Waugh
Andy Weekes
Yonathan Weitzman
Neil White
Lewis Whyld
Kirsty Wigglesworth
Phil Wilkinson
Sarah Williams
Les Wilson
Jim Winslet
William Wintercross
Jamie Wiseman
Mark Wohlwender
Gavin Wright
Chris Young
Andrey Zadorozhny
Ronen Zvulun